And They Called Me Crazy

Carol Murray Hunter

Copyright © 2024 by Carol Murray Hunter. All rights reserved.

No part of this book may be used or reproduced in any manner whatsoever without written permission, except in the case of reprints within the context of reviews.

Sparrow Books Press
A division of Sparrow Books LLC
Clarion, PA
www.sparrowbooksclarion.com

ISBN: 979-8-9921380-0-9
Library of Congress Control Number: 2024952395

Cover design by Sarah Cummings, using photos taken by Hunter of his garden, one of his favorite places in the world.

SPARROW BOOKS PRESS

For Hunter, who gave me life beyond my wildest imagination. Thank you. You inspired me to write this, and I will forever hold on to the love we shared.

To anyone made to feel crazy for what others cannot understand: I see you.

Table of Contents

Introduction..3
and they called me crazy............................7

I. On Finding Him

Just Hunter.. 11
FLO RI DA!... 13
Lost Love.. 16
The Rapture of You...................................18
Sad Clown..20
Stick Man...22

II. On Finding Myself

Water off Vaseline..................................... 25
Looking Out...27
Searching for Flight: Attempts.................28
Upside Down Flowers...............................36
Another Sleepless Night........................... 37
Dreamer's Mind...39
Walls.. 41
The Other Part of Me................................ 43

Birds Of Prey 45

Insanity 47

Thoughts of Imagination 49

Inner Self 51

First Winter in the Woods 52

Face 55

REMEMBER 57

and I could call you crazy, too 59

Don't Leave Me 60

III.   On Losing Him

Without You 65

Spirit in the Night 66

A Pittsburgh Guy 67

An Artist in the Woods 69

Flower 70

His Beauty, My Beast 71

Shall I Start From the Beginning? 72

Dear Reader,

First, thank you. For picking up this collection, for opening yourself up to my story. I've had this story stirring inside of me since I was a little girl, laying in bed in my grandma's apartment under the watchful eye of her Mother Cabrini — the patron saint of immigrants — and crying because everytime she closed the door after tucking me in, I swear that statue lit up for me. This was before my grandma told me that I didn't need to cry, that I had a special gift and shouldn't fear it.

Here's what you need to know about me: for all my life, I've had vivid dreams, visions in my sleep, spirits that would visit me in the night. I've always considered myself clairvoyant, to which they'd all say — my mom, dad, siblings, friends — *stop talking so crazy*.

Growing up in the cold water flats in the Brooklyn projects, I learned young to be observant. Had to be, to stay out of trouble (although I still found my fair share). I always interpreted my surroundings naturally, could pick up on things they didn't want me to know, didn't think I could see. At school, I wore fishnet stockings, tight skirts, jewelry up and down my arms, glitter on my nose. My friends, they'd all say, *you look so crazy*.

I liked to stand out in a crowd, dance and feel wild. An artist, creating pieces my family couldn't understand. A rebel of the time, I didn't like rules, didn't like control. I was emotionally confused, abused. My first marriage was a nightmare I didn't know how to wake up from. My family didn't believe what I shared.

And so I curled in on myself. I began to doubt my own reality, hid what I saw in my dreams and what I experienced while awake.

And then in my twenties: the car crash. I was dead on arrival, almost fully decapitated. I saw the light, but they brought me back. Never quite the same: my vocal cords were paralyzed, the words gritty and lodged in my throat. But, even when I couldn't trust my voice — I could write.

It was a few years after that I first met Hunter. On a trip to visit friends in Florida, my first time out of New York. There he was. Spiritual in his own right, he embraced me, believed me. The one person who never made me feel crazy.

This, reader, is where these poems were born from. After the decades of manipulation, of fear, my nervous breakdown, every voice outside my head telling me I was being crazy, to be less, to hide myself — Hunter made me feel understood. Their word, *crazy,* still follows me, but I began to embrace it. And as Hunter and I moved through life together, what was once seen as crazy became understood, became right.

These poems span the entirety of our life together. Some written in the Florida heat during those wild, early days in the 70s; some written after our move to West Virginia; some written during the late, frigid nights when snow covered the trees outside our Leechburg home after moving back to his home state of Pennsylvania; some written after his death in 2021, when I feel his spirit in the flowers, reaching, waiting for me.

-Carol

and they called me crazy

they call me crazy
a long time ago.
Crazy Carol was the word below
a very long
time ago.

begin, begin
now — anew
but it was said,
a long time ago.

lost memories,
words flew through me,
now they are spilling out.
slime, slime
left me in time, like the
slime, slime, slime.
water flows through me with
time, time, time.

2021

I.

Just Hunter

I know a man
he's just Hunter —
for that is his name.
Can't give you no answers,
but I do wonder —

A street man he once was,
sold hoarded junk, and drank all that hard stuff.
But at the time, this was the answer,
for he is just Hunter.

He'd love them, leave them, and send them astray;
he was lost himself
and couldn't find the way.
For he is just Hunter.

On his own ever since he was three,
remembers every bit, he could have died eternally.
Life, and he is different in so many ways —
for now he is happy, and finally free.

His roads were rough and long,
but things don't come easy, just singing a sad song.
No, his is not sad, could never give in to such a drag,
for he is just Hunter.

Such a man of unique talents,
just being Hunter.
So happy now, is he — for he has met
his compatibility.
I know this man, just Hunter, now there can never
be another.
His eyes so beautifully shaped,
his distinct features of strength and insight.
Felt him from the first time we spoke.
It was just Hunter — Only just,
Hunter.

1976

FLO   RI   DA!

An empty place
is where I found you,
Alone, all by yourself,
and I – with someone else.
I saw you then, so alive and afraid to be
just you,
In Flo ri da!

Before my eyes, one fine day
appeared a hunter: green t-shirt, blue suede clogs.
An image beyond imagination for my eyes to see
Where?
In Flo ri da!

Just You,
a face so strong and distinct.
To look deep into his heart was to find his real soul
Where?
In Flo ri da!

We talked and talked, I was
mesmerized.
I belonged to you, then
but, did not know how to reframe.
For I was with that someone else
and you was by yourself.

This all happened last April
Where?
In Flo ri da!

    She cried when she left
    for her heart was left with him.
    Her body – in another land
    where she did not belong.

    He was left all alone in Indian Rocks Beach,
    at the end of the pier he would stare,
    into an empty night of empty tears.
    But, not knowing how she felt
    for she, in another land.

    She would send her soul to him
    through mail,
    only to hope that one fine day
    he would get the message.
    Where?
    God damn!
    In Flo ri da!

    She finally went to her man,
    Yes!
    Right down to Flo ri da.
    Packed child and all,
    she loved him so

couldn't wait to see him at the airport,
in their new land:
Flo ri da!

And
from then on
we've been one,
and a little one in between.
We all fit each other to a T,
Yeah!

My man wears t-shirts and I wear jeans,
do anything we goddamn please.
Love and get wild, cause
we are free
and the one in between?
She just fits the seams.

And just to think how it all started
I won't say
cause you already know.
You fool, how could you forget?
It all happened in the place called

FLO RI DA!

1976

Lost Love

A lover lost is a lover found.
I sent him away one fine day,
sweet thoughts of memory
are on my mind.
Visions of him in my dreams
seem to reappear, occasionally.

Loss of a friend,
a childhood love,
it's a shame it all had to end.

Womanly instinct led me away
it led me far, far from his sight.
I return to him through his visions,
but I am nowhere in sight.

I can see him
smiling through his tears
in my dreams at night.

A childhood love,
flowers that withered in mud,
are all left behind.

It's a shame we were such good friends,
lovers right down until the end,

childhood sweethearts, now come to its final end.
A love lost, a lover found.
A lover, lost.
A lover, found.

1977

The Rapture of You

The rapture of you
can only cling in the spirits of my mind
long lost in time.
Can time bring back loving?

The rapture of you.

Can love be found, or is it really lost forever?
Forever lost, yes, sometimes forever.
Denying love, memories of life and love
can turn into hate – never.

The rapture of you.

Dreams of passion linger in my soul and mind,
coldness in my heart,
or, is it the ego of past dreams?
Life and love cannot revolve around schemes.

The rapture of you.

Loving moments, the time we spent
seem to have turned into dented bents
bents of broken dreams, bents of the past –

The rapture of you.

The rapture of you
can only linger in my soul
for my heart is broken,
pieces of dreams.

The rapture of you!

1977

Sad Clown

For you, the only thing left

Today I am the sad clown,
frustration is upon my clouded windows of time.
Future goes on and days pass by quickly,
solitude can no longer be an escape.
Pass through my mind and let me see,
Happiness, Love, and Prosperity.
Visions of dreams, become my reality!

Stardom lingers in my brain,
but today I am the sad clown,
for you see –
today it has rained, a harsh downpour.
Tomorrow I will smile and paint my face with joy,
dance, sing and pretend to be free.
For I know what's down deep, deep inside of me.
Tears of losing battles beneath my mind and soul,
tears of sad clowns appear before my eyes.

But You!
You who sees laughter and joy upon my face.
You, who sees my faces of reality,
beyond the face that wears society –
you see me.

Someday I will be the image,
the image you see, deep down inside of me.
Someday that sad clown
will be free.

1977

Stick Man

Thunder and lightning we shall see and hear
before there is calm on the stormy seas.
A Red Stick Man figure I do see,
felt something strange when I painted thee.
An artist can only paint what they feel
but, that Red Stick Man figure meant something to
me.

His glitter eyes that shined in the night,
followed you everywhere with shimmering lights.
He was angry,
and so was me,
so we rode along that stormy sea.
The thunder and lightning was there, too
but it will pass, for storms usually do.

The flowers glistened with sheer delight,
for they alone told that the future was bright.
The colors of purple and maize, scarlet red and blue
meant all different expressions in my head.
The Stick Man, he shines his light now,
for the lightning has once begun.
The separation between the two is closing tight
together now, and will be forever.

1976

II.

Water off Vaseline

The mud and the gunk
is running off me like
Vaseline. Now!
No stick.

The rage of storms
flow, they run through me
like fireflies, lighting the sky.
Water runs
through me! For sure,
the dirt has left,
the path is clear!
The truth will flow,
my cup
runneth over.

No Fear!

Nothing can –
no dirt, no water – can
stick to me.
I am vaseline.

The path is clear,
water flows through me —

No fear!

We need the rain,
it's been dry —
Water is life to grow.
Wisdom is to be believed,
twilight, twilight.

The Hunter
always says,
Listen, listen to the wind.
Just listen.
Listen
Listen.

2009

Looking Out

I'm inside looking out, through the windows of my
vivid imagination.
Thoughts of future and past, pass in time
a year has gone — Ha! It went so fast!
Journeys have taken me for a rough ride.
I must rest now, for some fuel.
So tired and so much desired, all at the same time.
When will this rough ride end at last?

My body wears a sacred life's refrain,
it's beginning to show with time – although I am so
young to have this disguise.
It feels depressing, after a while.

Energy of a child, appear upon my clouded
windows,
they're getting blurry now.
Lights of the city shine elsewhere,
and I must shine too.
My vivid imagination takes care of that,
for I shall shine when I feel fit.
Gold must tarnish before it is bright,
And me … the difference is, I can come to life.

1977

Searching for Flight: Attempts

I.

Dreamer prevailing through sorrow
which binds, hurts, and has the blues,
Poor Child,
forsaken a happy life,
Poor Child.
It stings her heart through dreams at night.

Eyes so big and warm and brown,
raven black hair that shines so bright,
Poor Child,
it sure hurts to feel.

Feel the misery of defeat
feel the rain of empty nights,
Alone,
Poor child,
Alone.

II.

Away, away my little darling,
into the lonely night.
Fly on your wings of misery, yes,
fly free into the midnight.

So young and innocent, a child of doom.
Alone she must find her way.
Alone she must find her life.

In such deep solitude, all to herself.
Away, away my little darling,
away you must go,
see what life's about,
how it stings and claws at your brain.
See the hurt, feel the pain.
The pain of being alone, not knowing your way.
Feel this evil society, all stinkin' wet,
no money, no food.
Conquering the fears,
fears of just keeping yourself alive.
Feel the strive to hang on to life.

Away, away my little darling,
but, please, don't let yourself be hurt.
Away, away you must go.

III.

The blues torment a lady's heart
but she cannot say why.
Moments that should be beautiful
turn into darkness amongst the stars.
Blues set in and torment the mind,

tear away at the heart,
and linger in my soul.
Most of us feel this way,
but we cannot say why.

Words become unspoken,
love is delayed,
and days of future pass on in time.
In my mind, it is not there for me to say.

Away, away, fly,
yes, fly.
Escaping reality that is visionless to me,
entering a world of free illusion.
Illusions of stars and the sea.
Night, become my destiny.
Reality, please – let me
be free!

The blues torment a lady's heart.
But why?
Life beyond the sky,
can't we see?

Free, free –
I try,
to be free.

IV.

Words of wisdom I can hear
deep in the night,
become life,
become my world.
Words of wisdom, spread my wings
let me be free, free to be me.

Wisdom is exceptionally rational,
thoughts flow through patterns of time,
rhythms of musical sounds soothe a frustrated mind.
Visions of eternity prevail in my brain,
Wisdom…
Such a wise word to curtail.
Freedom, fly, fly, free,
wrap yourself around the universe,
content with wisdom.
Be free, free to be me.

Life goes on, days fly by
fly, fly, free.
Oh wisdom, let me be free,
free to be me.

V.

Lady, today you have a broken wing.

Let me mend and soothe your heart
place gardenias in your hair,
and give you a gown that
flows with musical sounds.
Mend your wing, and give you
new life that sings...

I will hold you tight
and swing you aloft, on top of Freedom Mountain.
Lady, don't be so sad,
for I can mend your broken wing,
I will let you fly, through misty clouds of gold,
place diamonds at your feet,
you will shimmer in the darkness of each and every
night.

My Poor Darling Lady, with your
Poor Broken Wing,
accept my gentle gift of soothing visions.
Clouds above you, I will take away,
and drift them out to sea.
I will surround you in ecstasy and beautiful
thoughts,
yes, soon your broken wing will shine,
dance, and sing…

Do I see tears before My Lady's eyes?

Oh how sad! Such big tears in My Lady's alluring eyes,
so sad!
You will not allow your broken wing to mend.
Give me your wings, and place them
in my ruthless mind,
visions escaping your eyes.
Soon, My Lady, you will dance and sing,
hold me, hold me, ever so tight.
Hold me, hold me, you must fight, fight,
Fight!!

It's all over now,
you may fly above the heavens.
Go, My Lady, go,
escape, Lady, your broken wing,
it is all mended.
Go wander, My Lady, wander
beyond Freedom Mountain.
Spread your wings across the heavens skies.
Fly, My Lady, fly…
Fly free.

VI.

She appeared before me,
an image of pure delight,

the total essence of sweet smelling beauty all about her

Intrigue me with your smile of death.
Entice me with your everlasting life.

The valley beneath her a bottomless pit,
whirlpools of fire sprayed with mist,
allusions of beauty prevailing upon her face

Who are you?
Image of ravishing delight.

She disappeared before my eyes,
left me to myself.
Devastating vibrations she left behind her,
flew off into eternity like a falcon of prey

Why did you go away?

Left me behind with a tingling sensation,
the alluring movement of her expression
frightened me as she fled.

Away! Away! My lady spread your wings,
blossom with life,
fly free, fly concealed in the midnight.
Aloft, on top of the world,
let your eyes see.

Feel me. Envision me.

Like appaloosas running wild,
spread your wings of flight,
journey on into the night.

Away, away.

I awoke as she disappeared,
sadness in my eyes,
alone, alone.

Escaping the thoughts as my eyes arose,
my mind alerted to the feelings of reality.
It's ended, my fantasy,
she's gone.
But,
her vision remains, with me.

1977 – 1987

Upside Down Flowers

Tears of loneliness
fill my eyes.
Tears of emptiness
fill my heart.
Lost for positive thoughts
beautifying my mind,
Where am I now?
Who am I today?
Tomorrow will be a brighter day,
Or – will it be like yesterday?

Upside down flowers I can see
for in real life, it is only fantasy,
but in my mind, it's reality.

I am so lost
for beautiful thoughts,
for my man has now left it up to me.
Tears of emptiness fill my heart.
Tears of loneliness fill my soul.

1976

Another Sleepless Night

Sleepless nights of emptiness and frustration,
when will it end?
At times I feel as if I want to die,
things must change soon for me.
An Artist with no picture, A Poet with no name,
I feel as if that should be my name.

Endless days of unforeseen journeys,
I must move continuously.
If only there were someone I could call,
I wouldn't feel like my life was at a downfall.

The moon is very strange this month, you see,
not like that of before.
Something is stirring around the earth.
Why do I feel this way?

Life's expectations of no conscious state,
it is the subconscious mind we want,
we must fill our head with positive thoughts
for our souls must not wander away.

Sleepless nights of emptiness and frustration
will be rewarded greatly someday,
in our next lives of energy.
Not like the one before,

or like that of old yesterdays.

1976

Dreamer's Mind

To live a life this simply divine,
is the ideal thing for the dreamer's mind.
For this does not and cannot exist.
It's total life's reality that we shall kiss.

To feel its pain and sorrow,
but desire only an everlasting fire,
fire that sometimes will go out,
but in the dreamer's heart,
no one can play the part.

To understand life's total meaning
and to find peace within its doors,
doors in which fashion open and close —
for it is you, yourself that can have any meaning,
you have the choice to choose how it can be controlled.

Only the dreamer can see and feel
the everlasting desire
they were gifted to behold.

Behold the gift of being uniquely divine.
For it is only the dreamer
that will touch and feel that desire,
desire to create and rebirth life's meaning

into a world of their own,
one in which alien cannot enter,
a world in which no one can understand.

For that is left to the imagination and mind
of only the dreamer...

1976

Walls

Within these walls I follow you.
To where,
I do not know.
Upon the walls that surround me day by day
are broken dreams that have withered away.
Life beyond the wall,
I cannot see,
but in return the walls, they can see me.
Paintings to hide the feelings of claustrophobia.
Paintings to me which are alive.

Within these walls I follow you.
I'm looking for an escape.
Eyes upon me, walls can only see,
follow you, follow you every day, every night
to where? I do not know.
Abstract art is everywhere in sight.
It's my world.
It's my life.

Go now, go now,
go beyond the wall.
It's just illusion,
just an illusion.

Go now, go now,

go beyond the wall,
but be real careful not to fall.

1977

The Other Part of Me

Wake up your adrenaline, it's been asleep.
Where have you been, Child ..?
This is not you in this mask of self pity.
It's another part of you.

Look at me – to you I look the same.
But what I see affects my mind and lingers in my brain.
Wild and wonderful, bizarre and obsolete
why do you act so meek?
Cry out! Cry Out!   Boo hoo, Hoo,
This gift I sent, is it not good for you?

Stay, you are not so strange.
Don't let self doubt fool you.
Wisdom of adaptation has appeared in your mind.
Let it pass and live on.
Fear is not an answer, self-reassured,
it is a wall, right in front of you.

Jump over, over the wall.
Don't be afraid to fall.
Cause when you land,
there is an Up.

So Look Up, Look Up.

1977

Birds Of Prey

Birds of Prey I do see today
as for yesterday, it has gone away.
Thoughts and visions I can see
far, far away,
could there be that land of eternity?

In my mind, which
moves so fast,
flashes of color I can see,
colors of seasons –
spring, winter, fall,
all autumn colors.
Summer days have been long gone,
the snowflakes are all that's left in my mind.
Leaves turning their color,
colors of the season.

Birds fly high
to keep their strength,
Birds fly low, where their time has descended.
But as life goes by,
day by day,
thinking of those yesterdays, all gone away.
For today,

today we are the Birds of Prey.

1976

Insanity

My life is at the epitome of defeat,
roads that were filled with promising dreams have
long gone away,
shadows of unforeseen passing surround a
temperamental heart.
Bewilderment and obsession of failure
perk beneath the pillow at night

    SEARCHING, SEARCHING

Astonishing, beholding eyes look upon me.
Closets bearing memories of more sensual days
have wilted like a flower.
Cry Out!
Clutch your fingers and plead for some peace.
Insanity has taken a greater part of me.
Endless nights dazed by thoughts of conquest

    SEARCHING, SEARCHING

Promising dreams have long gone away,
bloated, ugly and old, and all dried up.
A clown without his makeup is just an average face.
It's the makeup on the clown that makes you laugh
and smile,
just like music makes you sing.

Fear hangs out
in the super-ego of the mind.
Id has shattered through confinement, ego lost,
confusion destroyed by astonishing patterns of
frustration

      SEARCHING, SEARCHING

1977

Thoughts of Imagination

Thoughts beyond your imagination,
only fantasies.
For one, they are an escape,
to another, their fantasies are reality,
but for me — thoughts are free.

Orange skies, purple maize clouds, all lined in gold,
flowers forever blooming, never a day of endless doom.
You can let your body float round and round,
a world of beautiful gifts.
To look upon the sea
and feel its life force.
To journey beyond the tide
and see silver puffs of clouds.
A silver moon glittering and gleaming to give life to an empty night,
let it fill your lonely midnight.

Imagination is a rare and unique gift:
your thoughts can always wander.
Look upon a branch and feel it come to life.
Touch a flower, feel its soft and gentle sweet smell
of life blooming free,
without hesitation or fear.
A wild song, do let your ears hear.

Nature gives us flowing patterns of imagination,
all in itself,
its beautifying thoughts, they're left up to you.

Fly about the sky like a bird in flight,
let your inner self go,
be alive and live your dreams,
be free and flowing as the sunlight,
be a swan of purest white
let your beak be bright golden yellow,
the water beneath you aqua green
above, a glistening sun of fire orange,
doves flying all about you,
casting shadows of their baby blue wings.
Imagine sounds of wind breezing gently,
hear the harp play when it turns to night.

It's all there, and it doesn't cost a cent.
All it takes is your free and alert thoughts,
deep in your imagination.

1977

Inner Self

Sooner or later there will come my day,
the day I've cherished in all my journeys.
Life beyond the sky, I can feel and see,
but it happens to me quite constantly.

Die, die, visions escape the mind.
Life here is quite strange to me.
Live and love, and will not
die in poverty.

Sooner or later, there will come my day,
now or never, can you accept my reality?
Words unwritten in your ear,
now maybe you will hear.
The inner self, exploited.
It will be.
Can you see?

1987

First Winter in the Woods

      I.

Frozen Palace

I looked within your walls,
and saw a diamond palace.
Your world, so frozen
and cold.
I saw your arms, bent
and withered,
calling for spring.

But your palace of ice,
it seemed to cry
with shimmering grief.
Beneath your arms,
catacombs appear
entwined to your lover.

The lover cries, and
her tears
turn to melted ice.
For soon, she will blossom with love.

To me,
your palace was such a sight,

so untouched by reality,
so frozen with life.

I cry for you, and yes!
I do cry for me.
So beautiful your powers seem to be,
so frozen with ecstasy.
Can you see,
Can you see,
Can you feel me?

    II.

Roads of Beautiful Ice

Wandering through the misty starlit roads,
free like the wind through the atmosphere,
my eyes can envision beautiful colors of spring.

But reality arises at the sense of sleepiness,
beauty, can it be, so cold and dead?
Icicles form and linger in my head.

Coldness, fearless to the earth.
In darkness, life comes alive,
shimmering, glistening, before an endless flight.

The side of the road, your branches stretch,

frozen.
Through the woods,
catacombs appear entwined.

Starlit roads, their
fingers drip icicles.
Soon there will be life here.

If death shall be so raptured,
then shall life be so well formed?

Within the earth's seasons,
my eyes are finding freedom.
Colors follow denial, how I made my escape:
coldness, fearless to the earth.

Beautiful frozen eyes,
glittering, sparkling.
Hesitate not, wait not for spring.
But live, live now
as these roads of beautiful ice.

1988
Leechburg, PA

Face

Upon my face of sorrow, happiness and confusion,
dismay can only be upon my lips.
But may my eyes see brighter days of future.

It has rained upon my palace this month,
changes are everywhere in sight.
Confusion clouds my windows,
the wind surrounds my world and mind.
But, the sun will shine on my parade.
Day by day we change.

It has been a heavy one,
yet I still see the light shining in
through the windows of my mind.
There is need to be stronger, much stronger,
life in the past is over.

Reality does not strike at the door.
It's hard when your life has shattered its nerves to death.
But love can put back the missing pieces.

Fear can only destroy a goal in life.
I can no longer be fearful of the future.
Whatever, whatever, it will be,
there is nothing you can do but to make it better.

Yes!

1977

REMEMBER

To Hunter – the only thing that is left for you to do is Remember me! I will be somebody someday! I will.

Remember me in time!
Remember me as the future goes by.
Remember life? When it wasn't so hard
And all that was important was fun.
Remember me…

Remember the words from within my soul,
Words of my life, my heart, my mind.
Being young wasn't so hard,
Remember me…

Days go by and life goes on
Fighting each day away.
Hours are like candles that have melted in time,
Remember me,
But remember,
Remember me…

Me, who was lost a long long time ago,
And still I'm here to go on,
Remember me..!

Colors of rain appears before my eyes,
Colors of time, of future, and colors of past,
But can you remember me,
Please.
Remember Me...

1977

and I could call you crazy, too

crazy, me?
for wanting to be free,
always wanting to be free.
for talking to spirits in the night,
but I know they are alive in my heart,
in my mind.

for loving someone as deep as the ocean, as high as the sky.
one who lives in another space and another time.

waiting and waiting (that's me!)
for the one who waits.
the saint peter of the Indian saints.
because, yes, I'm gonna meet him at those gates.

so they might call me crazy,
but yeah – you know what?
we're all a little crazy.

Oct 15th, 2024
Happy Birthday, Hunter

Don't Leave Me

Don't leave me now,
don't leave me ever.
But can we live together?
Life gets tougher every day.
I love you, but can we live together?

Children of past lives linger in our hearts and soul –
we were made for each other.
Can we find a place in time
to forgive the past?
Give us a future that will last.

Don't leave me now,
don't leave me ever.
But can we live together?

You are you and I am me,
can we find a place to be together,
      Forever?

Joys of passion that fill my mind and soul,
have drifted into the winds of time.
Can we ever bring them back,
or do we throw them in a potato sack,
only to rot and remember what we once had,
only to turn sour and bad?

Don't leave me now,
don't leave me ever.
But can we live together?
Only to forget the past.
Only to go on, to make it last!

1987

III.

Without You

What do I do!
Don't know how to live
Without you.
Just an artist in the woods
trying to find that life,
Without you.

Lost, lost trying to
find you in the night.
Lost, lost, trying to find
my brain in the light.
Be still, till I find my sight.

You're a squirrel
in front of my house,
running across a wood log.
You're my animal spirit
in the sky, in the daylight, and
into the night –
and I am here,
Without you.

2021

Spirit in the Night

To the one who waits —
I want you, need you, oh god,
too stubborn to die.

I love you as deep as the ocean, as high as the sky.
You have to walk through fire to get by.

To the one who waits —
I am a vision before you,
Timeless.

Oh, he took me with him when he died,
and he is waiting,
For me!
Timeless.

2024

A Pittsburgh Guy

One Christmas,
my parents gave me a blue transistor radio
that I would listen to
in my room, at night.

I would listen to, Porky Chedwick,
Daddio of the Radio,
Platter Pushing and Poppa,
Pork the Tork.

He would play
all the oldies,
and it was coming from Pittsburgh,
where he would talk.

It was the 60s,
the world was young,
and so was I.
Little did I know,
years later,
that I would meet
A Pittsburgh Guy.

He would be from Pittsburgh,
with a name I always dreamed of having.

The man of my dreams,
the man of my soul —
Hunter.

2024

An Artist in the Woods

That's me!
I want to dance with you,
I want to party, party,
party with you,
dance until the morning light,
screamin' into the night.
Love, love, love ya
till I can't come home.
Love love love ya
till you bring me home.

2021

Flower

The only flower beyond the wood log in front of
my house,
it has to be you.
There in the woods – it can only be
you.
Before me, behind me, in front of me, around me.
It can only be you.

Surround me in ecstasy
until I can hear your voice in the wind.
Mind reading, read my mind!
My mind will be yours!
And your mind will be mine.

2021

His Beauty, My Beast

He was my beauty,
he was my beast.
I was his beauty,
and he was my beast.

I was his queen of the night
and queen of his day.
And he was my king,
my savior, my
everlasting love.

I was forever his beauty
and he is
forever —
my beast.

2021

Shall I Start From the Beginning?

It's my first Thanksgiving
without you in my life.

Black Friday, the first snow of the season,
into the beginning
of the darkest part of my life
without you —
for you no longer have life.

And I am here,
lost and alone,
depending on people,
and trapped,
with memories of you, only you —
without you.

Shall I start from the beginning?

He walked into the room
in his hunter green t-shirt,
his navy blue suede clogs.
Straight into the room he walked,
and sat in that space, right next to me.

And we looked into each other's eyes
and we knew —

we were in love, and we'd never be lost.

He said to me —
Do you know how beautiful you are
And I said —
That's a good line
I was in love.
And he was in love.
It was the beginning
of a new journey for me.
And they called him —
Just Hunter.

2021

Acknowledgements

Thank you to Sarah: my editor, cover designer, and publisher. Thank you for listening to me and believing in me. You helped me accept what I wrote, and I couldn't have gotten here without you.

Thank you so much to Jo for taking the time to read and provide feedback on this collection, and for validating my story.

I am forever grateful to my friends and family for supporting me all my life. To my siblings who have been there for me through thick and thin: my brother for always being there, and my sister for listening to me everyday. To my daughter for being there for me and giving me strength when I most needed it, and to my granddaughter for helping me when times were at their worst.

And I am eternally grateful to my granddaughter for finding the original copies of these poems. Missing for over thirty years, I thought I had lost them in one of our moves. But then, on the night of Hunter's death, my granddaughter went looking for something in the barn and came back with a folder stuffed thick with pages: these poems, waiting for me.

And thank you, of course, to Hunter, for giving me all this life to put on the page.

Made in United States
North Haven, CT
12 January 2025

63487620R00052